wit & wisdom
from the

Zen
Masters

13-Digit ISBN: 978-1-60433-994-9
10-Digit ISBN: 1-60433-994-2

This book may be ordered by mail from the publisher. Please include $5.99 for postage and handling. Please support your local bookseller first!

Books published by Cider Mill Press Book Publishers are available at special discounts for bulk purchases in the United States by corporations, institutions, and other organizations. For more information, please contact the publisher.

Cider Mill Press Book Publishers
"Where good books are ready for press"
PO Box 454
12 Spring Street
Kennebunkport, Maine 04046
Visit us online!
cidermillpress.com

Typography: Tomarik, Gloss Drop, Mrs. Eaves, Filson Soft
Image Credits: All images courtesy of Shutterstock.com

Printed in Singapore
1 2 3 4 5 6 7 8 9 0
First Edition

wit & wisdom
from the

CIDER MILL
PRESS

BOOK
PUBLISHERS
KENNEBUNKPORT, MAINE

Table of Contents

WHAT IS ZEN?

Zen is both what we are and what we do. It is the expression of our true nature and a disciplined practice celebrating the joy of being. There is no Zen doctrine or dogma one must undertake. It is a direct experience of ultimate reality. Zen is boundless. It is beyond words and intellect. Zen is not about beliefs or ideas, but universal wisdom that we can all discover in our daily lives. Through meditation, we can realize that self and other are One. It is a practice of vigilance and self-discovery.

Zen is known as the meditation school of Buddhism. Zazen is a form of seated meditation at the very heart of Zen practice. It is the study of the self—the Buddha sat in meditation under the Bodhi tree for forty-nine days to achieve enlightenment and to recognize the unity of the self and all things. Zazen is a way of realizing the non-dualistic, interconnected nature of all life. It blends the body, breath, and mind into one inseparable reality. For about 2,500 years, this meditation tradition has been passed down in India, China, Japan, and other parts of Asia before arriving in the West. Zen is not just a form of Buddhism, but a practice with universal relevance.

ON THE ESSENCE OF ZEN

Zen is an effort to become
alert and awake.

—Osho

Zen in its essence is the art of seeing into the nature of one's own being, and it points the way from bondage to freedom. By making us drink right from the fountain of life, it liberates us from all the yokes under which we finite beings are usually suffering in this world.

—D. T. Suzuki

The practice of Zen is forgetting the self in the act of uniting with something.

–Koun Yamada

Zen teaches nothing; it merely enables us to wake up and become aware. It does not teach, it points.

— D.T. Suzuki

Zen is not an art, it's not a religion. It's a realization.

—Gene Clark

There is no need for temples; no need for complicated philosophy. Our own brain, our own heart is our temple; the philosophy is kindness.

—Dalai Lama

Clouds come from time to time-
and bring to men a chance to rest
from looking at the moon.
—Matsuo Bashō

ON THE PRESENT MOMENT

AND MINDFULNESS

Happiness is when what you
think, what you say, and what you
do are in harmony.
—Mahatma Gandhi

This is the real secret of life—to be completely engaged with what you are doing in the here and now. And instead of calling it work, realize it is play.
—Alan Watts

The only thing that is ultimately real about the journey is the step that you are taking at this moment. That's all there ever is.

—Eckhart Tolle

I'm here to tell you that the path to peace is right there, when you want to get away.

—Pema Chödrön

THINGS DERIVE THEIR BEING AND
NATURE BY MUTUAL DEPENDENCE
AND ARE NOTHING IN THEMSELVES.

—NĀGĀRJUNA

When you are present,
you can allow the mind
to be as it is without getting
entangled in it.
—Eckhart Tolle

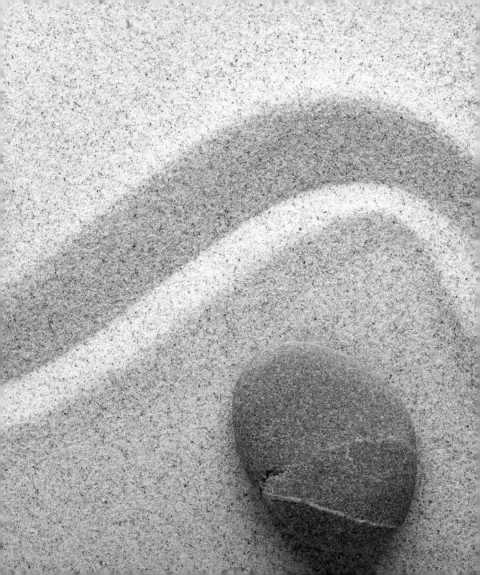

Be the change that you want to see in the world.

—Mahatma Gandhi

Practice is this life,
and realization is this life,
and this life is revealed
right here and now.

❧ ● ❧

—Maezumi Roshi

If you want to change the world, start with the next person who comes to you in need.

—B.D. Schiers

Wherever you are, be there totally.

—Eckhart Tolle

Throughout this life,
you can never be certain
of living long enough to
take another breath.

—Huang Po

The art of living… is neither careless drifting on the one hand nor fearful clinging to the past on the other. It consists in being sensitive to each moment, in regarding it as utterly new and unique, in having the mind open and wholly receptive.

—Alan Watts

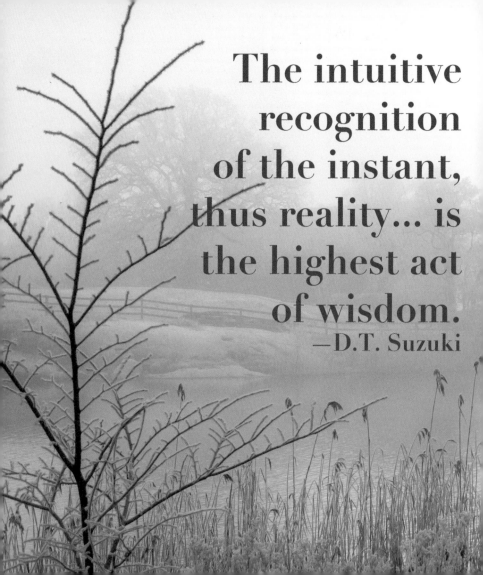

The intuitive
recognition
of the instant,
thus reality... is
the highest act
of wisdom.
—D.T. Suzuki

Nothing ever exists entirely alone.
Everything is in relation to everything else.
—Buddha

THE SAME ROOT, THE TEN-THOUSAND
THINGS, AND I ARE OF ONE SUBSTANCE.

❧ ❧

—SÊNG-CHAO

Guilt, regret, sadness, and all forms of nonforgiveness are caused by too much past and not enough present.

—Eckhart Tolle

TO LIVE—
IS THAT NOT
ENOUGH?

—D.T. SUZUKI

Roads were made
for journeys not
destinations.

—Confucius

We are here to awaken from our illusion of separateness.

—Thích Nhat Hanh

Nature does not hurry, yet everything is accomplished.
—Lao Tzu

How admirable,
He who thinks not, "Life is fleeting,"
When he sees the lightning!
—Matsuo Bashō

ON TRUE SELF AND NO SELF

The practice of Zen is forgetting the self in the act of uniting with something.

—Koun Yamada

I don't let go
of concepts—I
meet them with
understanding.
Then they let go
of me.

—Byron Katie

If you forget yourself, you become the universe.

—Hakuin Ekaku

The Zen expression "Kill the Buddha!" means to kill any concept of the Buddha as something apart from oneself.

—Peter Matthiessen

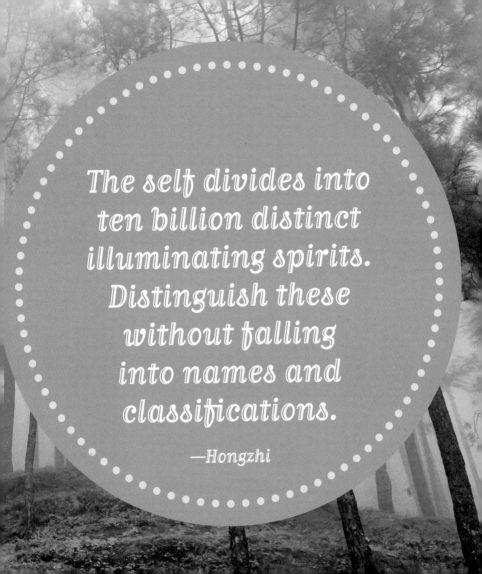

The self divides into ten billion distinct illuminating spirits. Distinguish these without falling into names and classifications.

—Hongzhi

To study Buddhism is to study the self. To study the self is to forget the self. To forget the self is to be awakened by all things.
—Dogen Zenji

Have good trust in yourself... not in the One that you think you should be, but in the One that you are.

— Taizan Maezumi Roshi

Melting our attachment to self is the most powerful medication for bringing mental and emotional imbalances in check.

—Dzigar Kongtrul Rinpoche

Knowing others is intelligence; knowing yourself is true wisdom. Mastering others is strength; mastering yourself is true power.

—Lao Tzu

It is easy to believe we are each waves and forget we are also the ocean.

—Jon J. Muth

WE WILL BECOME WHO WE ARE MEANT TO BECOME.

— MAHATMA GANDHI

Now I know
what success is:
living your truth,
sharing it.

—Kamal Ravikant

When you do something,
you should burn yourself up
completely, like a good bonfire,
leaving no trace of yourself.
—Shunryu Suzuki

ON DIRECT EXPERIENCE

Zen has no business with ideas.

❧ ✤ ☙

—D.T. Suzuki

My finger can point to the moon,
but my finger is not the moon. You
don't have to become my finger, nor
do you have to worship my finger.
You have to forget my finger, and
look at where it is pointing.

—Osho

The world is its

own magic.

—Shunryu Suzuki

What is important is
not the right doctrine
but the attainment of
the true experience.
It is giving up
believing in belief.

—Alan Keightley

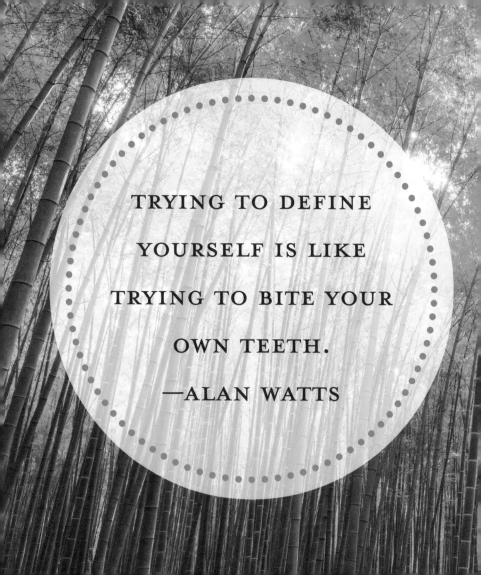

TRYING TO DEFINE
YOURSELF IS LIKE
TRYING TO BITE YOUR
OWN TEETH.
—ALAN WATTS

Don't try to steer the river.

—Deepak Chopra

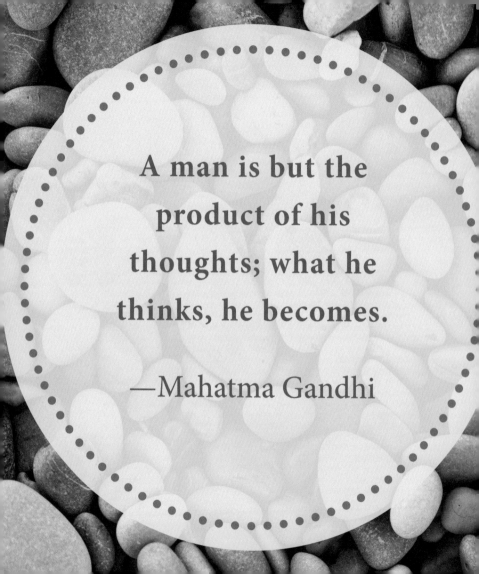

A man is but the product of his thoughts; what he thinks, he becomes.

—Mahatma Gandhi

A man is great not because he hasn't failed; a man is great because failure hasn't stopped him.

— Confucius

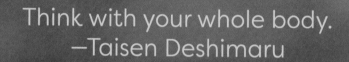
Think with your whole body.
—Taisen Deshimaru

I write, erase, rewrite,
Erase again, and then
A poppy blooms.
—Hokushi

ON ZEN IN EVERYDAY LIFE

One must be
deeply aware of the
impermanence of
the world.

—Dogen Zenji

When an ordinary man attains knowledge, he is a sage; when a sage attains understanding, he is an ordinary man.

—Zen Proverb

Today, you can decide to walk in freedom. You can choose to walk differently. You can walk as a free person, enjoying every step.

—Thích Nhat Hanh

Flow with whatever may happen and let your mind be free: stay centered by accepting whatever you are doing. This is the ultimate.

❧ … ❧

—Chuang Tzu

NOBODY CAN HURT ME
WITHOUT MY PERMISSION.
—MAHATMA GANDHI

Let go over a cliff, die completely, and then come back to life—after that you cannot be deceived.

—Zen Proverb

Each step along the Buddha's path to happiness requires practicing mindfulness until it becomes part of your daily life.

—Henepola Gunaratana

Let your mind wander in the pure and simple. Be one with the infinite. Let all things take their course.
—Chuang Tzu

Only when you can be
extremely pliable and
soft can you be extremely
hard and strong.

—Zen Proverb

To understand everything is to forgive everything.
—Gautama Siddhartha

ANY ENLIGHTENMENT WHICH
REQUIRES TO BE AUTHENTICATED,
CERTIFIED, RECOGNIZED,
CONGRATULATED, IS FALSE, OR AT
LEAST INCOMPLETE.
—R. H. BLYTH

Self-realization is effortless. What you are trying to find is what you already are.

—Ramesh Balseka

The aim of spiritual life is to awaken a joyful freedom, a benevolent and compassionate heart in spite of everything.

— Jack Kornfield

This dewdrop world—
It may be a dewdrop,
And yet— and yet.
—Matuso Bashō

ON THE TRUE NATURE

OF THINGS

You are a function of what the whole universe is
doing in the same way that a wave is a function
of what the whole ocean is doing.

—Alan Watts

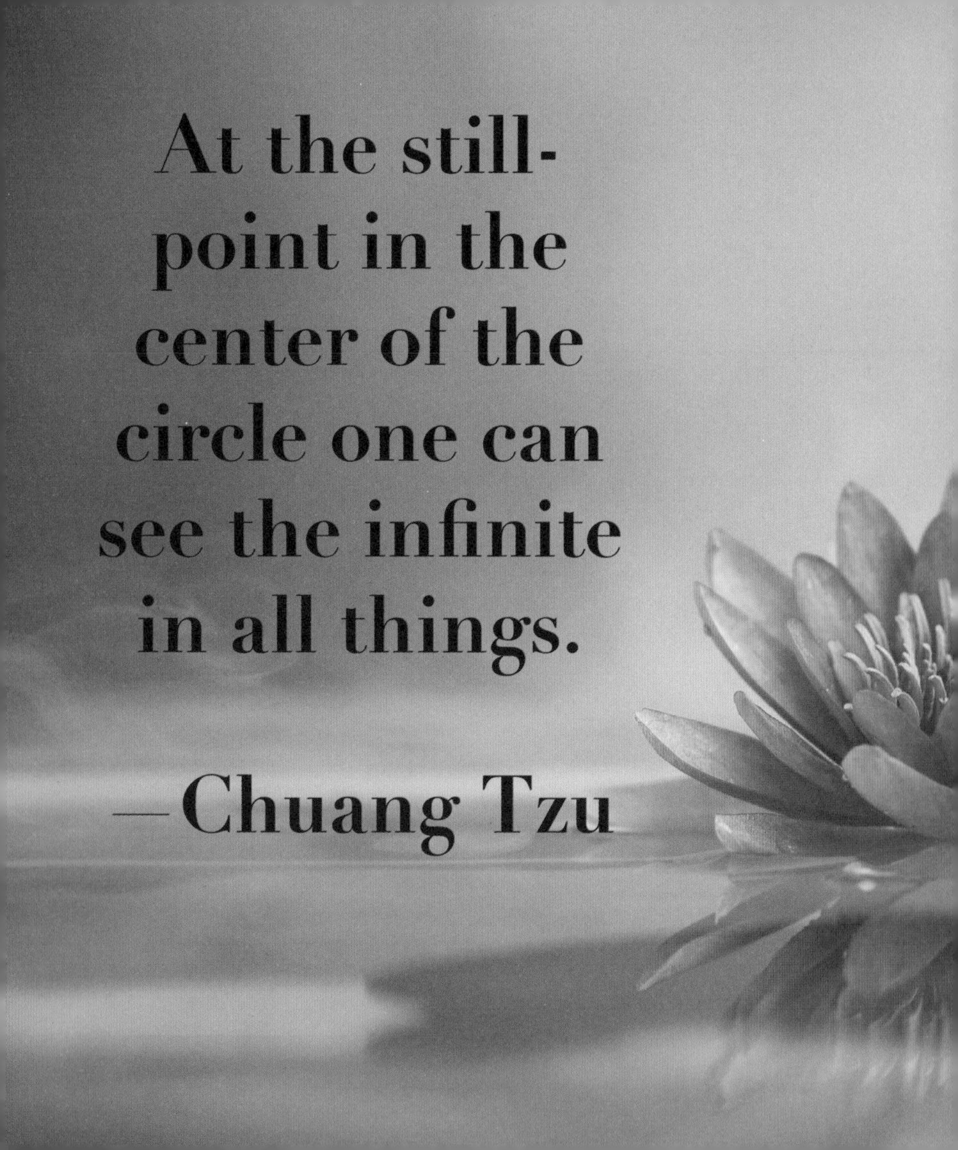

At the still-
point in the
center of the
circle one can
see the infinite
in all things.

—Chuang Tzu

In the scenery of spring,
nothing is better, nothing worse;
The flowering branches are
of themselves, some short, some long.

—Toyo Eicho

NO
SNOWFLAKE
EVER FALLS
IN THE
WRONG
PLACE.

—ZEN PROVERB

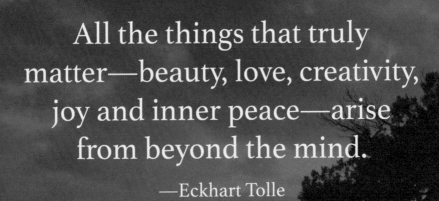

All the things that truly matter—beauty, love, creativity, joy and inner peace—arise from beyond the mind.

—Eckhart Tolle

Through our eyes, the universe is perceiving itself. Through our ears, the universe is listening to its harmonies. We are the witnesses through which the universe becomes conscious of its glory, of its magnificence.
—Alan Watts

Out beyond ideas
of wrongdoing and
rightdoing there
is a field. I'll meet
you there.

—Jalal al-Din Rumi

Do not seek the truth, only cease to cherish your opinions.

—Seng-ts'an

Things are as they are. Looking out into the universe at night, we make no comparisons between right and wrong stars, nor between well and badly arranged constellations.

—Alan Watts

No thought, no reflection, no analysis, no cultivation, no intention; let it settle itself.
—Tilopa

As a bee gathering nectar does not harm or disturb the color and fragrance of the flower, so do the wise move through the world.
—Buddha

The evening haze;
Thinking of past things,
How far-off they are!
—Matsuo Bashō

ON NON-STRIVING AND THE WAY

The search
for happiness
is one of the
chief sources of
unhappiness.

— Eric Hoffer

The resistance to the unpleasant
situation is the root of suffering.
—Ram Dass

MAN SUFFERS ONLY BECAUSE HE
TAKES SERIOUSLY WHAT THE GODS
MADE FOR FUN.
—ALAN WATTS

These mountains
that you are carrying,
you were only
supposed to climb.

—Najwa Zebian

FOR THINGS TO REVEAL THEMSELVES TO US, WE NEED TO BE READY TO ABANDON OUR VIEWS ABOUT THEM.

—THÍCH NHAT HANH

If you are unable to find the truth right where you are, where else do you expect to find it?

—Dogen Zenji

The meaning of life is just to be alive. It is so plain and so obvious and so simple. And yet, everybody rushes around in a great panic as if it were necessary to achieve something beyond themselves.
—Alan Watts

Life isn't as serious as the mind makes it out to be.

—Eckhart Tolle

The greatest effort is not
concerned with results.

—Atisha

Act without expectation.
—Lao Tzu

Muddy
water is best
cleared by
leaving it
alone.

— Alan Watts

When mind exists undisturbed in the Way, nothing in the world can offend, and when a thing can no longer offend it ceases to exist in the old way. When no discriminating thoughts arise, the old mind ceases to exist.

— Seng-ts'an

The more
you know,
the less
you need.

—Yvon Chouinard

Out of nowhere the mind comes forth.

—from the Diamond Sutra

ON ZEN LIVING

Zen is not some fancy, special art of living. Our teaching is just to live, always in reality, in its exact sense. To make our effort, moment after moment, is our way. In an exact sense, the only thing we actually can study in our life is that on which we are working in each moment. We cannot even study Buddha's words.

—Shunryu Suzuki

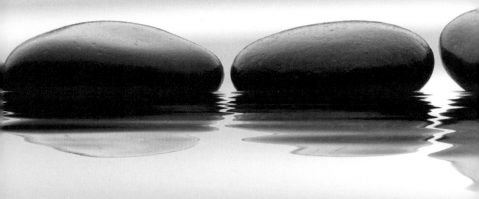

When we discover that the truth is already in us, we are all at once our original selves.

—Dogen Zenji

Zen is a liberation from time. For if we open our eyes and see clearly, it becomes obvious that there is no other time than this instant and that the past and the future are abstraction without any concrete reality.

—Alan Watts

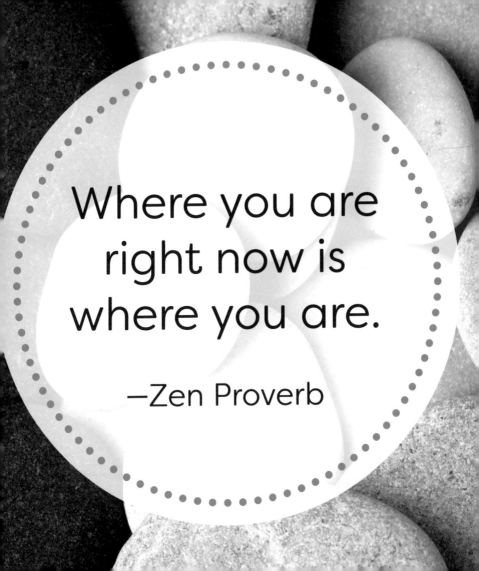

Where you are
right now is
where you are.

—Zen Proverb

To seek is to suffer. To seek nothing is bliss.

—Bodhidharma

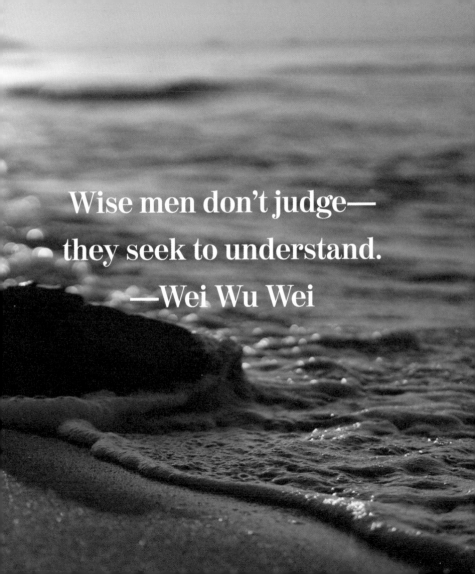

Wise men don't judge—
they seek to understand.
—Wei Wu Wei

I live by letting things happen.

–Dogen Zenji

Life is a balance
of holding on and
letting go.

—Jalal al-Din Rumi

Every experience is a lesson. Every loss is a gain.

—Sathya Sai Baba

Life begins where fear ends. —Osho

When one first seeks the truth, one separates oneself from it.
—Dogen Zenji

Love all.
Serve all.
Help ever.
Hurt never.

—Sathya Sai Baba

Our sorrows and wounds are healed only when we touch them with compassion.
—Buddha

It always seems
impossible until
it's done.

—Nelson Mandela

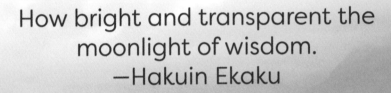

How bright and transparent the
moonlight of wisdom.
—Hakuin Ekaku

Treat every moment as your last. It is not preparation for something else.
—Shunryu Suzuki

About Cider Mill Press Book Publishers

Good ideas ripen with time. From seed to harvest, Cider Mill Press brings fine reading, information, and entertainment together between the covers of its creatively crafted books. Our Cider Mill bears fruit twice a year, publishing a new crop of titles each spring and fall.

"Where Good Books Are Ready for Press"

Visit us online at
cidermillpress.com
or write to us at
PO Box 454
12 Spring St.
Kennebunkport, Maine 04046